GCSE
English Language

SET A

Paper 1

Time allowed: 1 hour 45 minutes

For this paper, you will need:
- The **text**, which is provided in a separate insert.

Instructions to candidates
- Answer **all** the questions in the spaces provided.
- Write your answers in **black** ink or ball-point pen.
- Write your name and other details in the boxes below.
- Cross out any rough work that you do not want to be marked.
- You need to refer to the insert booklet for this exam.
- You should **not** use a dictionary.

Information for candidates
- The marks available are given in brackets next to each question.
- There are 80 marks available for this exam paper.
- **Section A** will test your reading skills and **Section B** will test your writing skills. There are 40 marks available for each section.
- You must use good English and clear presentation in your answers.

Advice for candidates
- You should spend about **15 minutes** reading through the text and all five questions.
- Make sure you leave enough time to check your answers at the end of the exam.

Centre name						Surname	
Centre number						Other names	
Candidate number						Candidate signature	

This product does not include any official AQA questions and is not endorsed by AQA.

Exam Set ENAP42

© CGP 2025 — copying more than 5% of this paper is not permitted

Section A: Reading

Spend about 45 minutes on this section.

You should answer **all** the questions in this section.

1 Use **lines 1-7** of the text to answer the questions below.

For each question, tick the correct option. There is one correct answer per question.

1.1 What does the author think a traveller would remember the Solomon valley for?

The sand bars ☐
The muddiness ☐
The emptiness ☐   **[1 mark]**

1.2 According to the writer, how does the river feel about the Solomon valley?

The river is indifferent about the valley ☐
The river dislikes the valley ☐
The river finds the valley boring ☐   **[1 mark]**

1.3 What does the writer note about the river's current?

It is slow ☐
It is strong ☐
It varies in speed ☐   **[1 mark]**

1.4 What does the writer think of the river?

It is just like other rivers ☐
It is too long ☐
It is useless ☐   **[1 mark]**

2 Explain how the writer uses language to describe the Solomon Valley in **lines 8-18**.

You may wish to explore how the writer uses particular language techniques, specific words and phrases, or different types of sentence.

[8 marks]

Leave blank

3 Write about how the writer has structured this text to create a sense of hopelessness.

In your answer, you could consider how a sense of hopelessness increases or decreases throughout the text, and any changes in tone or viewpoint.

[8 marks]

4 How far do you agree or disagree with the following statement?

*From **line 19 to the end** of the text, the writer makes the reader feel sympathy for Colonel Bywaters.*

In your answer, make references to the text and consider:

- what impression you get of Colonel Bywaters
- what methods are used to describe his life in El Dorado.

[20 marks]

Leave blank

Section B: Writing

Spend about 45 minutes on this section of the paper.
You are advised to plan your answer.
Write in full sentences.
Leave enough time to check your work.

5   You are writing a piece for a creative writing competition that will be judged by a local author. Choose **one** of the following tasks:

Write a description of an isolated place.
If you wish, you can use the photo below for inspiration.

OR

Write the beginning of a story based on the prompt 'alone in the wilderness'.

[40 marks]

....

....

....

....

....

Leave blank

END OF QUESTIONS

[Blank Page]

GCSE English Language

SET A

Paper 2

Time allowed: 1 hour 45 minutes

For this paper, you will need:
- **Text A** and **Text B**, which are provided in a separate insert.

Instructions to candidates
- Answer **all** the questions in the spaces provided.
- Write your answers in **black** ink or ball-point pen.
- Write your name and other details in the boxes below.
- Cross out any rough work that you do not want to be marked.
- You need to refer to the insert booklet for this exam.
- You should **not** use a dictionary.

Information for candidates
- The marks available are given in brackets next to each question.
- There are 80 marks available for this exam paper.
- **Section A** will test your reading skills and **Section B** will test your writing skills. There are 40 marks available for each section.
- You must use good English and clear presentation in your answers.

Advice for candidates
- You should spend about **15 minutes** reading through the texts and all five questions.
- Make sure you leave enough time to check your answers at the end of the exam.

Centre name					Surname	
Centre number					Other names	
Candidate number					Candidate signature	

This product does not include any official AQA questions and is not endorsed by AQA.

Exam Set ENAP42

© CGP 2025 — copying more than 5% of this paper is not permitted

Section A: Reading

Spend about 45 minutes on this section.

You should answer **all** the questions in this section.

1   The statements below are about **lines 1-15** of **Text A**.

   Tick the boxes next to the **four** statements that are TRUE.

   A   Martin Bright's journey took three and a half hours. ☐

   B   Martin Bright was unhappy about the delay to his flight. ☐

   C   Martin Bright felt the airport was a good place to relax while he was waiting for his flight. ☐

   D   Martin Bright began to think about how comfortable and relaxing travelling on the TGV would be. ☐

   E   Martin Bright was told that some of the delay should be made up during the flight. ☐

   F   Some of the passengers on the plane had problems with their seats. ☐

   G   Martin Bright got a free meal on his flight. ☐

   H   The plane landed at half past two in the morning. ☐

   [4 marks]

2 In **Text A** and **Text B**, the writers are describing their travel experiences.

What are the differences between travelling by stagecoach and travelling by aeroplane?

You need to:

- **infer** information from the text
- talk about **both texts** in your answer.

[8 marks]

3 Explain how the writer uses language to make the reader feel as though they are journeying on the stagecoach with him in **lines 1-15** of **Text B**.

[12 marks]

4 This question is about **Text A** and **Text B**, where both writers present their views and experiences of train travel.

Compare how they convey their different attitudes to train travel.

You may wish to explore what the writers' attitudes are and what methods they use to convey their attitudes. You should use examples from **both** texts.

[16 marks]

Leave blank

Section B: Writing

Spend about 45 minutes on this section of the paper.
You are advised to plan your answer.
Write in full sentences.
Leave enough time to check your work.

5 Write an article for a broadsheet newspaper arguing your opinion on the statement below.

'Aeroplane travel is bad for the environment and unnecessarily dangerous. More people should use other forms of transport for long-distance journeys.'

[40 marks]

Leave blank

END OF QUESTIONS

[Blank Page]

GCSE
English Language
SET A

Insert

Paper 1 (page 2):

- **Text — 20th-Century fiction**

  An extract from the short story *El Dorado: A Kansas Recessional* by Willa Cather.

Paper 2 (pages 3-4):

- **Text A — 21st-Century non-fiction**

  A newspaper article called *Is the journey really better by train?* by Martin Bright and Vanessa Thorpe.

- **Text B — 19th-Century literary non-fiction**

  An extract from *The Innocents Abroad*, a travel writing book by Mark Twain.

Acknowledgements
Paper 1, Text: Abridged and adapted text from El Dorado: A Kansas Recessional, by Willa Cather
Paper 2, Text A: © Guardian News & Media Ltd 2025
Paper 2, Text B: Abridged and adapted text from The Innocents Abroad, by Mark Twain

Exam Set ENAP42

Paper 1 Text — 20th-Century fiction

This extract is from the opening of a short story by Willa Cather, which was published in 1901. In this section the author describes the Solomon Valley in Kansas, a state of the USA, and the old man who lives there.

El Dorado: A Kansas Recessional

PEOPLE who have been so unfortunate as to have travelled in western Kansas will remember the Solomon valley for its unique and peculiar desolation. The river is a churning, muddy little stream, that crawls along between naked bluffs*, choked and split by sand bars, and with nothing whatever of that fabled haste to reach the sea. Though there can be little doubt that the Solomon is heartily disgusted with the country through which it
5 flows, it makes no haste to quit it. Indeed, it is one of the most futile little streams under the sun, and never gets anywhere. Its sluggish current splits among the sand bars and buries itself in the mud until it literally dries up from weariness and ennui**, without ever reaching anything.

Beyond the river with its belt of amber woodland rose the bluffs, ragged, broken, covered with shaggy red grass and bare of trees, save for the few stunted oaks that grew upon their steep sides. They were pathetic little
10 trees, that sent their roots down through thirty feet of hard clay bluff to the river level. They were as old as the first settler could remember, and yet no one could assert that they had ever grown an inch. They seldom, if ever, bore acorns; it took all the nourishment that soil could give just to exist. There was a sort of mysterious kinship between those trees and the men who lived, or tried to live, there. They were alike in more ways than one.

Across the river stretched the level land like the top of an oven. It was a country flat and featureless, without
15 tones or shadows, without accent or emphasis of any kind to break its vast monotony. It was a scene done entirely in high lights, without relief, without a single commanding eminence to rest the eye upon. The flat plains rolled to the unbroken horizon vacant and void, forever reaching in empty yearning toward something they never attained.

Near the river was a solitary frame building, low and wide, with a high sham front***, like most stores in
20 Kansas villages. Over the door was painted in faded letters, "Josiah Bywaters, Dry Goods, Groceries and Notions." In front of the store ran a straight strip of ground, grass grown and weedy, which looked as if it might once have been a road. Here and there, on either side of this deserted way of traffic, were half demolished buildings and excavations where the weeds grew high, which might once have been the sites of houses. For this was once El Dorado, the Queen City of the Plains, the Metropolis of Western Kansas, the coming Commercial
25 Center of the West.

Whatever may have been there once, now there were only those empty, windowless buildings, that one little store, and the lonely old man whose name was painted over the door. Inside the store, on a chair tilted back against the counter, with his pipe in his mouth and a big gray cat on his knee, sat the proprietor. His appearance was not that of the average citizen of western Kansas, and a very little of his conversation told you that he had
30 come from civilization somewhere. He was tall and straight, with an almost military bearing, and an iron jaw. He was thin, but perhaps that was due to his diet. His cat was thin, too, and that was surely owing to its diet, which consisted solely of crackers and water, except when now and then it could catch a gopher; and Solomon valley gophers are so thin that they never tempt the ambition of any discerning cat. If Colonel Bywaters's manner of living had anything to do with his attenuation****, it was the solitude rather than any other hardship
35 that was responsible. He was a sort of "Last Man." The tide of emigration had gone out and had left him high and dry, stranded on a Kansas bluff. He was living where the rattlesnakes and sunflowers found it difficult to exist.

The only human faces the Colonel ever saw were the starved, bronzed countenances of the poor fellows who sometimes passed in wagons, plodding along with their wives and children and cook stoves and feather beds,
40 trying to get back to "God's country." They never bought anything; they only stopped to water their horses and swear a little, and then drove slowly eastward. Once a little girl had cried so bitterly for the red stick candy in the window that her father had taken the last nickel out of his worn, flat pocketbook. But the Colonel was too kind a man to take his money, so he gave the child the money and the candy, too; and he also gave her a little pair of red mittens that the moths had got into, which last she accepted gratefully, though it was August.

Glossary
* bluffs — steep cliffs or banks
** ennui — boredom
*** sham front — a store front that's taller than the store itself
**** attenuation — thinness

Paper 2, Text A — 21st Century non-fiction

Is the journey really better by train?

The TGV* network now has a fast route to Marseilles. Vanessa Thorpe raced by train and Martin Bright by plane to the south of France. Who was first there — and who enjoyed it more?

Martin Bright — by plane

Three and a half hours into my journey to the south of France and I was still on British soil. The plane from Stansted had been delayed by 45 minutes and although I was still confident of beating the time taken to get to Marseilles on the TGV, I felt like I'd spent my whole morning travelling just to stand still.

However you look at it, airports are a rubbish place to spend even a second of your holiday and you can't concentrate on a book or genuinely relax over a croissant and coffee when you are waiting for a delayed flight. The whole point of flying is that it is supposed to be fast. With my frustration measured out in an ever-growing pile of Sunday supplements, I began to daydream about lying back in a comfy TGV seat with a big headrest and view of French vineyards.

We boarded the bee-yellow Buzz plane at about 11.30 amid assurances that we should be able to make up some time on the flight. The cabin crew were patient with niggles about the temperature being too cold (or too hot), seat cushions that had come free of their fastenings, seat backs that wouldn't go upright, and tables and arm rests that were awkward to use.

By now, I'd given up hope of lunch in Marseilles. But the in-flight salad (£3 extra) wasn't bad and it was clear that even this delayed flight was going to get me to Marseilles in good time. We touched down at 2.30pm, and after picking up a hire car I was on the road by three, just six hours after I left home.

There is no way of making the journey part of the holiday when you fly to the south of France, but it does get you there with hours to spare over the train. Thoughts of Stansted faded after I'd checked in to a hotel and had a glass or two in a café. I felt perfectly relaxed.

Vanessa Thorpe — by train

Train travel makes its initial appeal direct to my vanity. Somehow, no matter how organised I try to be, no matter how smart my luggage is or how freshly washed my hair, I always leave even the shortest aeroplane journey sallow, unkempt and out of control. Whether it is the scramble for the passport at the bottom of the bag, deciding what to pack away in the hold or the unpleasant paradox of seemingly having hours to wait and yet no time to relax, being 'processed' by an airport has always sapped my spirits and left me feeling a hostage to fortune.

So it was with visions of remaining neatly coiffed and accoutred** that I arrived at the Eurostar terminus at London's Waterloo ready to take the new train all the way to the South of France in record time — a promised six hours 50 minutes to Marseilles. I'd left my north London flat at the congenial hour of 11.30am so was easily able to check in for my 12.27pm departure ahead of the scary 20-minute cut-off point.

There is, we all know, a degree of stress involved in travelling anywhere, no matter how enticingly sunny the destination and easy the route, which is why the idea of a flying bed has always been one of my favourite fantasies. In the case of Eurostar, the sweaty palms and jolting starts to the traveller's heart are most likely to be caused by not finding the right escalator up to the right bit of the platform for the right coach of the train. Apart from that, once aboard, it really is fine to sit back and read, sleep, eat or drink — or all three. In the end it is pretty close to a flying bed really, except with nice scenery and a buffet service.

I pulled into Marseilles at 9.30pm, French time, half an hour late, but I was by now so relaxed that I scarcely noticed the delay. The journey from my door had taken me nine hours, but I felt as refreshed as if I had been lounging around on a sofa all day.

Travelling this way, I decided, connects you to the place you are going to in a way that is uniquely satisfying. Watching the landscape unravel, it is much easier to take pleasure in the differences. Arriving anywhere by plane is, in contrast, often disorienting and leaves you with aching ears and ballooned feet.

Of course, it still takes quite a bit longer to go by train, but you are on the move in the right direction the whole time, which I like. And I'd nearly finished my book.

Glossary

* TGV — a type of high-speed train   ** coiffed and accoutred — having hair and clothes arranged well

Paper 2, Text B — 19th Century literary non-fiction

In 1867, the American author Mark Twain travelled from New York to the Middle East, stopping at several other destinations along the way. This text is an extract from a travel writing book he wrote about his trip.

It is hard to make railroading pleasant in any country. It is too tedious. Stagecoaching* is infinitely more delightful. Once I crossed the plains and deserts and mountains of the West in a stagecoach, from the Missouri line to California, and since then all my pleasure trips must be measured to that rare holiday frolic. Two thousand miles of ceaseless rush and rattle and clatter, by night and by day, and never a weary
5   moment, never a lapse of interest! The first seven hundred miles a level continent, its grassy carpet greener and softer and smoother than any sea and figured with designs fitted to its magnitude — the shadows of the clouds. Here were no scenes but summer scenes, and no disposition inspired by them but to lie at full length on the mail sacks in the grateful breeze and dreamily smoke the pipe of peace — what other, where all was repose and contentment? In cool mornings, before the sun was fairly up, it was worth
10   a lifetime of city toiling and moiling to perch in the foretop with the driver and see the six mustangs** scamper under the sharp snapping of the whip that never touched them; to scan the blue distances of a world that knew no lords but us; to cleave the wind with uncovered head and feel the sluggish pulses rousing to the spirit of a speed that pretended to the resistless rush of a typhoon! But I forgot. I am in elegant France now. It is not meet that I should make too disparaging comparisons between humdrum
15   travel on a railway and that royal summer flight across a continent in a stagecoach. I meant in the beginning to say that railway journeying is tedious and tiresome, and so it is — though at the time I was thinking particularly of a dismal fifty-hour pilgrimage between New York and St. Louis. Of course our trip through France was not really tedious because all its scenes and experiences were new and strange.

The cars*** are built in compartments that hold eight persons each. The seats and backs are thickly
20   padded and cushioned and are very comfortable; you can smoke if you wish; there are no bothersome peddlers****; you are saved the infliction of a multitude of disagreeable fellow passengers. So far, so well. But then the conductor locks you in when the train starts; there is no water to drink in the car; there is no heating apparatus for night travel; if a drunken rowdy should get in, you could not remove a matter of twenty seats from him or enter another car; but above all, if you are worn out and must sleep, you must
25   sit up and do it in naps, with cramped legs and in a torturing misery that leaves you withered and lifeless the next day.

In France, all is clockwork, all is order. They make no mistakes. Every third man wears a uniform, and whether he be a marshal of the empire or a brakeman, he is ready and perfectly willing to answer all your questions with tireless politeness, ready to tell you which car to take, yea, and ready to go and put you
30   into it to make sure that you shall not go astray. But the happiest regulation in French railway government is — thirty minutes to dinner! No five-minute boltings of flabby rolls, muddy coffee, questionable eggs, and pies whose conception and execution are a dark and bloody mystery to all save the cook that created them! No, we sat calmly down and munched through a long table d'hote***** bill of fare, then paid the trifle it cost and stepped happily aboard the train again, without once cursing the railroad company.

Glossary
*   stagecoaching — travelling in a covered horse-drawn wagon
**   mustangs — wild horses
***   cars — railway carriages
****   peddlers — travelling salesmen
*****   table d'hote — a set menu with a fixed price

GCSE
English Language

SET B

Paper 1

Time allowed: 1 hour 45 minutes

For this paper, you will need:
- The **text**, which is provided in a separate insert.

Instructions to candidates
- Answer **all** the questions in the spaces provided.
- Write your answers in **black** ink or ball-point pen.
- Write your name and other details in the boxes below.
- Cross out any rough work that you do not want to be marked.
- You need to refer to the insert booklet for this exam.
- You should **not** use a dictionary.

Information for candidates
- The marks available are given in brackets next to each question.
- There are 80 marks available for this exam paper.
- **Section A** will test your reading skills and **Section B** will test your writing skills. There are 40 marks available for each section.
- You must use good English and clear presentation in your answers.

Advice for candidates
- You should spend about **15 minutes** reading through the text and all five questions.
- Make sure you leave enough time to check your answers at the end of the exam.

Centre name					Surname	
Centre number					Other names	
Candidate number					Candidate signature	

This product does not include any official AQA questions and is not endorsed by AQA.

Section A: Reading

Spend about 45 minutes on this section.

You should answer **all** the questions in this section.

1   Use **lines 1-8** of the text to answer the questions below.

For each question, tick the correct option. There is one correct answer per question.

1.1   Where is the trail?

Above the level of the forest floor ☐

Beneath the level of the forest floor ☐

At the same level as the forest floor ☐   **[1 mark]**

1.2   What is the trail covered in?

Mud ☐

Animal footprints ☐

Greenery ☐   **[1 mark]**

1.3   How does the writer describe the trail?

Wide ☐

Windy ☐

Narrow ☐   **[1 mark]**

1.4   What has pushed up the end of a rail?

A tree ☐

A spike ☐

A wooden plank ☐   **[1 mark]**

2   Explain how the writer uses language to describe the old man in **lines 9-16**.

You may wish to explore how the writer uses particular language techniques, specific words and phrases, or different types of sentence.

[8 marks]

3   Write about how the writer has structured this text to create a sense of danger.

In your answer, you could consider how a sense of danger increases or decreases throughout the text, and any changes in tone or viewpoint.

[8 marks]

4   How far do you agree or disagree with the following statement?

*From **line 17 to the end** of the text, the writer creates a vivid portrayal of the boy which makes the reader feel as though they know a lot about him and his life.*

In your answer, make references to the text and consider:

- what impression you get of the boy
- what methods are used to describe the boy.

[20 marks]

Leave blank

Section B: Writing

Spend about 45 minutes on this section of the paper.
You are advised to plan your answer.
Write in full sentences.
Leave enough time to check your work.

5 You are going to enter your school's creative writing competition. Your entry will be judged by a panel of your classmates. Choose **one** of the following tasks:

Write a description of a dangerous forest.
If you wish, you can use the photo below for inspiration.

OR

Write the beginning of a story based on the prompt 'an encounter with an animal'.

[40 marks]

Leave blank

Leave blank

END OF QUESTIONS

[Blank Page]

GCSE English Language

SET B

Paper 2

Time allowed: 1 hour 45 minutes

For this paper, you will need:
- **Text A** and **Text B**, which are provided in a separate insert.

Instructions to candidates
- Answer **all** the questions in the spaces provided.
- Write your answers in **black** ink or ball-point pen.
- Write your name and other details in the boxes below.
- Cross out any rough work that you do not want to be marked.
- You need to refer to the insert booklet for this exam.
- You should **not** use a dictionary.

Information for candidates
- The marks available are given in brackets next to each question.
- There are 80 marks available for this exam paper.
- **Section A** will test your reading skills and **Section B** will test your writing skills. There are 40 marks available for each section.
- You must use good English and clear presentation in your answers.

Advice for candidates
- You should spend about **15 minutes** reading through the texts and all five questions.
- Make sure you leave enough time to check your answers at the end of the exam.

Centre name					Surname	
Centre number					Other names	
Candidate number					Candidate signature	

This product does not include any official AQA questions and is not endorsed by AQA.

Section A: Reading

Spend about 45 minutes on this section.

You should answer **all** the questions in this section.

---

1 The statements below are about **lines 1-12** of **Text A**.

Tick the boxes next to the **four** statements that are TRUE.

- A   Miranda Sawyer thought that the butterfly bicycles were impressive. ☐
- B   Miranda Sawyer felt that James Bond's helicopter ride with the Queen was disappointing. ☐
- C   The ceremony celebrated what people can achieve together. ☐
- D   Tim Berners-Lee's words were shown on the sides of skyscrapers. ☐
- E   The ceremony reminded Miranda Sawyer of Glastonbury in the evening. ☐
- F   The torch was lit by seven retired athletes. ☐
- G   Each petal that created the torch represented a different country. ☐
- H   Miranda Sawyer had a strong emotional reaction to the lighting of the torch. ☐

[4 marks]

2   In **Text A** and **Text B**, the writers are each describing their experience of a public event.

What are the differences between the opening ceremonies of the 1851 Great Exhibition and the 2012 London Olympics?

You need to:

- **infer** information from the text
- talk about **both texts** in your answer.

[8 marks]

3 Explain how the writer uses language to describe the exhibition opening in **lines 3-29** of **Text B**.

[12 marks]

Leave blank

4 This question is about **lines 22-39** of **Text A** and the **whole** of **Text B**, where both writers are describing their experience of a busy public event.

Compare how they convey their different attitudes towards the events they describe.

You may wish to explore what the writers' attitudes are and what methods they use to convey their attitudes. You should use examples from **both** texts.

[16 marks]

Leave blank

Section B: Writing

Spend about 45 minutes on this section of the paper.
You are advised to plan your answer.
Write in full sentences.
Leave enough time to check your work.

5 Write a speech arguing your opinion on the statement below.
Your speech will be delivered during a school debate.

'Opening ceremonies for large events such as the Olympics are a waste of money. The money would be better spent making the actual events better for the people attending.'

[40 marks]

Leave blank

END OF QUESTIONS

[Blank Page]

GCSE
English Language
SET B

Insert

Paper 1 (page 2):

- **Text — 20th-Century fiction**

  An extract from the novel *The Scarlet Plague* by Jack London.

Paper 2 (pages 3-4):

- **Text A — 21st-Century non-fiction**

  A newspaper article containing two reviews of the 2012 London Olympics opening ceremony.

- **Text B — 19th-Century literary non-fiction**

  A diary entry by Queen Victoria.

Acknowledgements
Paper 2, Text A: © Guardian News & Media Ltd 2025
Paper 2, Text B: Supplied by the Royal Archives | © His Majesty King Charles III 2025

Paper 1 Text — 20th-Century fiction

This extract is from the opening of a novel by Jack London. It was published in 1912, but is set in the year 2073 after a plague has wiped out most of humanity. In this section, an old man and a boy are travelling through a forest.

The Scarlet Plague

The way led along upon what had once been the embankment of a railroad. But no train had run upon it for many years. The forest on either side swelled up the slopes of the embankment and crested across it in a green wave of trees and bushes. The trail was as narrow as a man's body, and was no more than a wild-animal runway.

5   Occasionally, a piece of rusty iron, showing through the forest-mold, advertised that the rail and the ties* still remained. In one place, a ten-inch tree, bursting through at a connection, had lifted the end of a rail clearly into view. The tie had evidently followed the rail, held to it by the spike long enough for its bed to be filled with gravel and rotten leaves, so that now the crumbling, rotten timber thrust itself up at a curious slant. Old as the road was, it was manifest that it had been of the mono-rail type.

An old man and a boy travelled along this runway. They moved slowly, for the old man was very old, a touch of
10   palsy** made his movements tremulous, and he leaned heavily upon his staff. A rude skull-cap of goatskin protected his head from the sun. From beneath this fell a scant fringe of stained and dirty-white hair. A visor, ingeniously made from a large leaf, shielded his eyes, and from under this he peered at the way of his feet on the trail. His beard, which should have been snow-white but which showed the same weather-wear and camp-stain as his hair, fell nearly to his waist in a great tangled mass. About his chest and shoulders hung a single, mangy
15   garment of goatskin. His arms and legs, withered and skinny, betokened extreme age, as well as did their sunburn and scars and scratches betoken long years of exposure to the elements.

The boy, who led the way, checking the eagerness of his muscles to the slow progress of the elder, likewise wore a single garment — a ragged-edged piece of bearskin, with a hole in the middle through which he had thrust his head. He could not have been more than twelve years old.

20   Tucked coquettishly over one ear was the freshly severed tail of a pig. In one hand he carried a medium-sized bow and an arrow. On his back was a quiverful of arrows. From a sheath hanging about his neck on a thong, projected the battered handle of a hunting knife. He was as brown as a berry, and walked softly, with almost a catlike tread. In marked contrast with his sunburned skin were his eyes — blue, deep blue, but keen and sharp as a pair of gimlets***. They seemed to bore into all about him in a way that was habitual. As he went along he
25   smelled things, as well, his distended, quivering nostrils carrying to his brain an endless series of messages from the outside world. Also, his hearing was acute, and had been so trained that it operated automatically. Without conscious effort, he heard all the slight sounds in the apparent quiet — heard, and differentiated, and classified these sounds — whether they were of the wind rustling the leaves, of the humming of bees and gnats, of the distant rumble of the sea that drifted to him only in lulls, or of the gopher, just under his foot, shoving a pouchful
30   of earth into the entrance of his hole.

Suddenly he became alertly tense. Sound, sight, and odor had given him a simultaneous warning. His hand went back to the old man, touching him, and the pair stood still. Ahead, at one side of the top of the embankment, arose a crackling sound, and the boy's gaze was fixed on the tops of the agitated bushes. Then a large bear, a grizzly, crashed into view, and likewise stopped abruptly, at sight of the humans. He did not like them, and
35   growled querulously. Slowly the boy fitted the arrow to the bow, and slowly he pulled the bowstring taut. But he never removed his eyes from the bear. The old man peered from under his green leaf at the danger, and stood as quietly as the boy. For a few seconds this mutual scrutinizing went on; then, the bear betraying a growing irritability, the boy, with a movement of his head, indicated that the old man must step aside from the trail and go down the embankment. The boy followed, going backward, still holding the bow taut and ready. They waited till
40   a crashing among the bushes from the opposite side of the embankment told them the bear had gone on.

Glossary
   *   ties — the wooden planks that the rail is attached to
   **   palsy — a term for medical conditions that can cause some body parts to shake
   ***   gimlets — sharp tools used for boring holes

Paper 2, Text A — 21st-Century non-fiction

In the article below, the journalist Miranda Sawyer and the singer Emmy the Great review the opening ceremony of the 2012 London Olympics for a broadsheet newspaper. The ceremony was directed by Danny Boyle, a well-known film maker.

London 2012: Opening ceremony — reviews

Miranda Sawyer: A collective vision

Horny-handed men of toil doing a Stand and Deliver* formation dance. Hundreds of NHS nurses combining to assist the birth of a giant glowing baby. Those amazing butterfly bicycles.

It seems daft to pick out individual elements of this great and glorious pageant — though James Bond's helicopter ride with the Queen was a proper "whoop whoop" moment — as Danny Boyle's vision was a deliberately collective one. He chose to celebrate what we can achieve together. When he picked out single people — Isambard Kingdom Brunel, Tim Berners-Lee, Mr Bean — it was to highlight what they gave to us all. Berners-Lee's words on the openness of the web, flashed around the stadium in letters the size of skyscrapers, was what this event was about. This Is For Everyone.

At times I was reminded of the Green Fields at Glastonbury** at 5am — the drums, the people, the benevolent united madness — and Danny Boyle's come-one-come-all attitude is very post-rave***. It extended right through to the lighting of the flame by seven young athletes and the petals of that flame, one for each competing country, coming together to form one enormous torch. A proper goosebumps moment, but just one among many.

The music section, though it sounded great, was the least successful visually, as a house flashing with images of Hugh Grant bibbling, of Renton**** running, just didn't seem all that thrilling after we'd had an enormous Voldemort growing before our very eyes. And there were a few weird omissions — no Oasis? Stone Roses? Primal Scream? Adele? — though, to be honest, they might have been in there but just whizzed past. To see Dizzee Rascal belt out Bonkers really did make me proud. That wouldn't have happened anywhere else.

The only bit that failed was good old Sir Paul McCartney: not because he's bad, but because he seems to have been singing Hey Jude in a stadium for the past five years. It felt slightly hackneyed, something we've seen before, and nothing else — absolutely nothing else — about this ceremony was anything other than original.

It was terrific, spectacular, moving, wonderful. Oh, the joy of people! It made me cry.

Emmy the Great: It made me addicted to patriotism

Like many Londoners, I've spent the last six months making an Olympic sport of complaining about the Olympics. Complaining, I felt, is what we do best, along with being cynical, unwelcoming to visitors, and a bit moany about traffic. All the bloody adverts! Giving directions to tourists! Those awful mascots. Danny Boyle was going to have to come at me with a wrecking ball to break down the barriers of uninterest that I had erected. And in a way he did. In fact, it's really hard writing this without the excessive use of capitals. I don't think I've ever felt quite such a bewildering mixture of true excitement and national pride over things I never really had an opinion on before, like Harry Potter, or Mr Bean, who had me weeping with laughter. During the runup I was aware that there are things about England that I am proud of. Not sport, really, but culture, and the NHS. To see this reflected on the screen during the opening ceremony actually blew my mind. I thought the NHS scene was incredibly brave, and I loved how much pop music featured. Whenever I travel, I am always aware of how our rich culture of great rock'n'roll affects people's opinion of us abroad.

I feel like Boyle got the tone right every step of the way. It was knowing, but sincere, dark and hilarious, like we are. And it was everything I needed to get excited about the next few weeks. By the end of the night, I was so addicted to patriotism I started cheering for countries that I'd visited, or that I'd once met someone from. It felt amazing.

I think all the medals should be melted down and made into one giant medal for Danny Boyle. They should just make him king of something. I feel like Kenneth Branagh in the industrial revolution scene right now, looking upon Britain with satisfaction and pride. Go team!

Glossary
* Stand and Deliver — a 1981 song by the band Adam and the Ants
** Glastonbury — a pop-music festival that takes place in Somerset in the summer
*** post-rave — influenced by rave music and culture (a type of electronic music played at energetic dance parties in the late 1980s and 1990s)
**** Renton — the main character in the film *Trainspotting*

Paper 2, Text B — 19th-Century literary non-fiction

This is a diary entry by Queen Victoria. In it, she describes attending the opening of the 1851 Great Exhibition, an exhibition of cultural and industrial items from around the world, jointly organised by her husband, Prince Albert.

This day is one of the greatest and most glorious days of our lives, with which, to my pride and joy the name of my dearly beloved Albert is for ever associated! It is a day which makes my heart swell with thankfulness.

The Park presented a wonderful spectacle, crowds streaming through it, — carriages and troops passing, quite like the Coronation Day, and for me, the same anxiety. The day was bright, and all bustle and excitement. At half past 11, the whole procession, in 9 state carriages, was set in motion. The Green Park and Hyde Park were one mass of densely crowded human beings, in the highest good humour and most enthusiastic. I never saw Hyde Park look as it did, being filled with crowds as far as the eye could reach. A little rain fell, just as we started, but before we neared the Crystal Palace*, the sun shone and gleamed upon the gigantic edifice, upon which the flags of every nation were flying. We drove up Rotten Roe and got out of our carriages at the entrance in that side. The glimpse through the iron gates of the Transept**, the waving palms and flowers, the myriads of people filling the galleries and seats around, together with the flourish of trumpets, as we entered the building, gave a sensation I shall never forget, and I felt much moved. In a few seconds we proceeded, Albert leading me; having Vicky at his hand, and Bertie*** holding mine. The sight as we came to the centre where the steps and chair (on which I did not sit) was placed, facing the beautiful crystal fountain was magic and impressive. The tremendous cheering, the joy expressed in every face, the vastness of the building, with all its decorations and exhibits, the sound of the organ (with 200 instruments and 600 voices, which seemed nothing), and my beloved Husband the creator of this great "Peace Festival", inviting the industry and art of all nations of the earth, all this, was indeed moving, and a day to live forever. God bless my dearest Albert, and my dear Country which has shown itself so great today. One felt so grateful to the great God, whose blessing seemed to pervade the whole great undertaking.

The Procession of great length began which was beautifully arranged, the prescribed order, being exactly adhered to. The Nave**** was full of people, which had not been intended and deafening cheers and waving of handkerchiefs, continued the whole time of our long walk from one end of the building, to the other. Every face, was bright and smiling, and many even, had tears in their eyes. One could of course see nothing, but what was high up in the Nave, and nothing in the Courts. The organs were but little heard, but the Military Band, at one end, had a very fine effect as we passed along. We returned to our place and Albert told Lord Breadalbane to declare the Exhibition to be opened, which he did in a loud voice saying "Her Majesty Commands me to declare the Exhibition opened", when there was a flourish of trumpets, followed by immense cheering. We then made our bow, and left. Everyone was astounded and delighted.

The return was equally satisfactory, — the crowd most enthusiastic and perfect order kept. We reached the Palace at 20 minutes past 1 and went out on the balcony, being loudly cheered. That we felt happy and thankful, — I need not say, — proud of all that had passed and of my beloved one's success. I was more impressed by the scene I had witnessed than words can say. Dearest Albert's name is for ever immortalised and the absurd reports of dangers of every kind and sort, set about by a set of people, are silenced. It is therefore doubly satisfactory that all should have gone off so well, and without the slightest accident or mishap. Phipps and Colonel Seymour***** spoke to me with such pride and joy, at my beloved one's success and vindication, after so much opposition and such difficulties, which no one, but he with his good temper, patience, firmness and energy could have achieved. Without these qualities his high position alone, could not have carried him through.

Glossary

*   Crystal Palace — the glass building specially built to house the Great Exhibition
**   Transept — the shorter arms of a cross-shaped building
***   Vicky and Bertie — Queen Victoria and Prince Albert's two eldest children
****   Nave — the main part of a building (usually a church)
*****   Phipps and Colonel Seymour — soldiers and courtiers who served Queen Victoria and Prince Albert

CGP

GCSE AQA
English Language

For exams in 2026 and beyond

Practice Exam Papers
Instructions & Answer Book

Exam Set ENAP42

Practice is the best way to prepare for the GCSE English Language exams...

...and this CGP pack will make sure you're totally ready — with two full sets of practice papers!

They cover every reading and writing skill on the AQA course and they're a great way to track your progress as you work towards the grade you want.

We've also included full mark schemes with sample answer points, making it easy to see where your strengths are — and which areas need a little extra work.

CGP — still the best! ☺

Our sole aim here at CGP is to produce the highest quality books — carefully written, immaculately presented and dangerously close to being funny*.

Then we work our socks off to get them out to you — at the cheapest possible prices.

*Admittedly these practice papers aren't very funny, since we were too busy concentrating on making them as serious as the real exams. But normally we'd include more jokes, honestly.

Using These Practice Papers

There are Two Sets of Practice Papers

This pack contains two sets of practice exams — **Set A** and **Set B**.
Each **set** is made up of **two separate papers**:

- Paper 1 is all about **fiction** texts.
- Paper 2 is all about **non-fiction** texts.

There's an **Insert Booklet** for each set, which contains the **texts** for Paper 1 and Paper 2.

For each paper, answer the questions under exam conditions, then **mark** them using this booklet. The questions here look a bit different to the ones you'll get in the **real exams**, but they'll still help you to get **prepared**.

How to Mark the Papers

You can **mark** these practice papers **yourself**, or you can ask **someone else** to mark them for you. This is often a good idea — it means you can get someone else's **opinion** of your work.

We've given you **marking grids** with **descriptions** of the **type** of answer that'll get you a certain number of marks. To mark each question, you need to:

1) Read through the marking grid and work out which **level description** fits the answer best.

2) Decide how **well** you think the answer **matches** the level description. If it only does **some** of the things mentioned, give it one of the lower marks in the level. If it does **everything** in the level **well**, you can give it a higher mark.

> Don't worry if you find it **tricky** using the **marking grids** at first. All answers are different, and it's unlikely that your answer will fit **all** the descriptions for a particular mark. It's just a question of finding the "**best fit**".

For each question, we've also provided some **examples** of **well-written points** you might find in a good answer. These can be used when marking to help judge the level of an answer, but remember — they're just **examples**. There will be lots of **other good points** that could be made.

After your answers have been marked, look at where you **lost marks**. That's the stuff you need to **learn**. Go away and **practise** these bits — then try **another paper** to see if you've improved.

Published by CGP

Editors: Emma Crighton, Rebecca Greaves, Delicia Ong and Matt Topping

With thanks to Kirsty Sweetman for the proofreading, and Jade Sim for the copyright research.

This product does not include any official AQA questions and is not endorsed by AQA.

Clipart from Corel®
Printed by Elanders Ltd, Newcastle upon Tyne.

Based on the classic CGP style created by Richard Parsons.

Text, design, layout and original illustrations © Coordination Group Publications Ltd. (CGP) 2025
All rights reserved.

Photocopying more than 5% of a paper is not permitted, even if you have a CLA licence.
Extra copies are available from CGP with next day delivery • 0800 1712 712 • www.cgpbooks.co.uk

How Did You Do?

- After you've done a complete exam (paper 1 and paper 2), use the answers and mark scheme in this booklet to mark each paper.

- Write down your marks for each paper in one of the tables below — each paper is worth a maximum of 80 marks.

- Find your total for the whole exam (out of a maximum of 160 marks) by adding up your marks from both papers.

- Follow the instructions below to work out your rough grade.

Set A							
Question	1	2	3	4	5	Total	Rough Grade
Paper 1							
Paper 2							
					Overall		

Set B							
Question	1	2	3	4	5	Total	Rough Grade
Paper 1							
Paper 2							
					Overall		

Estimating Your Grade

- If you want to get a **rough idea** of the grade you're working at, we suggest you compare the **total mark** you got in **each set** to the latest set of grade boundaries.

- Grade boundaries are set for each individual exam, so they're likely to **change** from year to year. You can find the latest set of grade boundaries by going to **www.cgpbooks.co.uk/gcsegradeboundaries**

- Jot down the marks required for each grade in the table below so you don't have to refer back to the website. Use these marks to **estimate your grade**. If you're borderline, don't push yourself up a grade — the real examiners won't.

Total mark required for each grade									
Grade	9	8	7	6	5	4	3	2	1
Total mark out of 160									

- Remember, this will only be a **rough guide**, and grade boundaries will be different for different exams, but it should help you to see how you're getting on.

Set A — Paper 1

Before you start marking the Set A, Paper 1 practice exam, have a look at page 3 — you'll find some handy advice about how to mark these practice papers. Make sure you've had a good read of it all before you get going.

Section A: Reading

1   1 mark for ticking each of the following correct answers:
    1.1 The emptiness
    1.2 The river dislikes the valley
    1.3 It is slow
    1.4 It is useless

2   When you're marking question 2, look at this table and work out which level description fits the answer best, then award the answer the mark you think it deserves from that level.

Number of marks	What's written	How it's written
7-8 marks Level 4	In-depth and insightful analysis of the effects of a variety of language features.	Sophisticated technical terminology is used accurately. A perceptive selection of references to the text are used to support points throughout.
5-6 marks Level 3	The effects of a selection of relevant language features are all clearly explained.	Technical terminology is used accurately throughout the answer. A variety of suitable references to the text are used to support points throughout.
3-4 marks Level 2	Some language features are identified and their effects commented on.	Some technical terminology is used. Might not always be accurate. Some relevant references to the text are used to support some of the points.
1-2 marks Level 1	Limited understanding of language features, with occasional comment.	Simple or no use of subject terminology. May be inaccurate. Few points are supported by relevant references to the text.
0 marks	Nothing written about language.	

Look for good points like these when you're marking:

- The writer uses adjectives such as "pathetic" and "stunted" to describe the trees in the valley. These words give the impression that the trees are starved and unable to grow much, which emphasises to the reader that the valley is almost lifeless. The reader might wonder how anything could survive in the valley if the trees struggle so much.

- The writer uses a simile, "like the top of an oven", to describe the land across the river. This image helps the reader to imagine just how "flat and featureless" the valley is by relating it to an object they would be familiar with. It also hints to the reader that, like an oven, the valley is uncomfortably hot.

- In the second paragraph, the writer uses a series of long, complex and repetitive sentences to imitate the monotony of the valley landscape. The monotony is reinforced by repetition of the word "without", which further emphasises how "vacant" the valley is.

- The writer uses personification to create an impression of the valley as a depressing place. For example, the flat plains are described as "forever reaching" towards something they cannot get. The idea that the plains themselves are "yearning" to leave, or in want of something that the valley can't provide, is an extreme way of demonstrating that nothing would want to exist here, and that it is a very hostile environment.

Set A — Paper 1

3   When you're marking question 3, look at this table and work out which level description fits the answer best, then award the answer the mark you think it deserves from that level.

Number of marks	What's written	How it's written
7-8 marks Level 4	Analyses the effects of a range of structural features confidently and in detail.	Sophisticated technical terminology is used accurately. Uses a perceptive range of examples from across the text.
5-6 marks Level 3	The effects of a variety of structural features are clearly explained.	Technical terminology is used accurately throughout. Suitable examples from the whole text are used and explained.
3-4 marks Level 2	The effects of some structural features are explained.	Some technical terminology is used. May not always be accurate Some points are supported with relevant examples from the text.
1-2 marks Level 1	Basic attempts to comment on a few structural features in a simple manner.	Simple or no use of subject terminology. May be inaccurate. Few references are made to the text and are not always relevant.
0 marks	Nothing written about structure.	

Look for good points like these when you're marking:
- The writer starts the text by giving a cinematic description of the wider scene: the river, the bluffs and the plains. The reader is immersed in the description of the whole desolate place. This establishes the hopelessness of the place, as it appears barren and lifeless. The desolation hints at the struggles of the character who will be introduced later.
- The focus then narrows down to the smaller, man-made aspects of the environment such as the "solitary" shop and the derelict settlement by the river. This increases the sense of hopelessness because the reader sees how "vacant and void" the place is. It is clear that humans have tried live on this land but for the most part have failed to do so.
- Finally, the text narrows down to a description of Colonel Bywaters and his "lonely" life. The writer uses a series of descriptions portraying the Colonel and his cat as "thin", due to their poor diets which stem from his "solitude". This series of sentences culminates in the short declaration "He was a sort of 'Last Man'", emphasising his hopelessness.
- The opening line and the final paragraph frame the extract by referencing the experiences of outsiders who have been "unfortunate" to have visited the area. The repeated suggestion is that outsiders do not find the place appealing and pass through quickly, which increases the sense of hopelessness as it highlights how the loneliness and desolation seem inescapable and is unlikely to ever change.

4   When you're marking question 4, look at this table and work out which level description fits the answer best, then award the answer the mark you think it deserves from that level.

Number of marks	What's written	How it's written
16-20 marks Level 4	In-depth, personal response to the statement, with critical, detailed analysis of the writer's choices.	Opinions are convincingly explained and fully supported with relevant, useful references to the text.
11-15 marks Level 3	Clearly explained response to the statement that discusses the effect of the writer's choices.	Opinions are clearly expressed and mostly supported with appropriate references to the text.
6-10 marks Level 2	An attempt at a personal response to the statement; some comments on the effect of the writer's methods.	Some opinions are explained and supported with references to the text.
1-5 marks Level 1	Limited response to the statement, with little mention of the effect of the writer's methods.	Only a few opinions are supported with relevant references to the text.
0 marks	Nothing written that responds to the statement.	

Look for good points like these when you're marking:
- I agree in some ways that the writer makes the reader feel sympathy for Colonel Bywaters. The writer shows the sense of destitution and abandonment in the town in which he lives by contrasting the "Queen City", "Metropolis" and "Commercial Center" of El Dorado in the past with the "deserted" and "half demolished" town of the present. This highlights the terrible state that the area is presently in, so the reader feels sympathy for anyone who is still living there.
- The writer also uses imagery to make the Colonel's life seem pitiful to the reader. For example, the metaphor "the tide of emigration had gone out and left him high and dry" creates an image of him as abandoned on an island, alone and unable to leave. This shows Bywaters' loneliness and suggests that he cannot escape his situation, making the reader feel sorry for him.
- However, some of the ways Colonel Bywaters is described make the reader feel less sympathetic towards him. The text says he has an "almost military bearing" and an "iron jaw", both of which suggest that he may have a staunch and stubborn personality. This hints to the reader that he is in his situation out of choice, and could leave if he wanted to.

Set A — Paper 1

Section B: Writing

5
- Question 5 tests two things. There are 24 marks for having an interesting and well-organised answer ('Ideas and structure'), and 16 marks for good technical accuracy, including spelling, punctuation and grammar ('Quality of writing').
- Mark each of the criteria separately, then add up the two marks to get a total out of 40.
- The best answers also need to be really well-matched to the form, purpose and audience that are specified in the question.

	Ideas and structure		Quality of writing
19-24 marks Level 4	Imaginative use of structure and language techniques, thoroughly matched to form, purpose and audience. Engaging, well-developed, sophisticated ideas in well-controlled paragraphs.	13-16 marks Level 4	Ambitious use of vocabulary with highly accurate spelling; confidently uses a wide range of grammar and punctuation.
13-18 marks Level 3	Effective writing, using a clear structure and language techniques. Matched to form, purpose and audience. Interesting, clearly connected ideas in organised paragraphs.	9-12 marks Level 3	Largely suitable, varied vocabulary with accurate spelling; a range of mostly correct grammar and punctuation.
7-12 marks Level 2	Mostly matched to form, purpose and audience. Some language techniques and structural features. A range of ideas in logical paragraphs.	5-8 marks Level 2	Attempts a variety of vocabulary, punctuation and grammar, sometimes successfully. Some accurate spelling.
1-6 marks Level 1	Some sense of form, purpose and audience, with a mostly disorganised structure. A few relevant ideas in poorly controlled paragraphs.	1-4 marks Level 1	Simple vocabulary, grammar and punctuation are used with inaccuracies throughout. Basic spelling may be correct.
0 marks	Nothing meaningful written.	0 marks	Poor spelling, grammar and punctuation, which prevents understanding.

Look for good techniques like these when you're marking:

In a description:
- Language that appeals to the senses: A chilly wind blew through the cracks in the decrepit door, grazing my cheeks, and a steady roll of thunder rattled from the sky.
- Similes: The tall hills and the glowering sky seemed as if they were preparing for a tempestuous battle.
- Personification: Only two stalwart sides of the ruined house remained, fighting bravely against the urge to fall. A pair of small, gaping windows peered forlornly out into the gloom.
- Descriptive words and phrases: Soft, plush grass, littered with buttercups, sprang up along both sides of the rough track.

In the beginning of a story:
- An interesting, dramatic opening sentence: I blindly fled across the moors, my heart racing, glancing behind me to check that I wasn't being followed.
- Plenty of detail to set the scene: There was nobody else around for miles — the only sounds were the whistling of the wind as it passed through the sparse, spindly trees and the crunching of the frosted grass beneath my feet.
- A good middle section that builds up to a key moment: I brushed the dense mulch of dirt and snow away and peered at the crumbled stone beneath, until I spotted some rough etchings — what did they mean?
- A final sentence that leaves an impression on the reader: Now, whenever I walk alone across those windswept moors, I quietly remember their incredible history, lost and forgotten for so many years.

Set A — Paper 2

Before you start marking the Set A, Paper 2 practice exam, have a look at page 3 — you'll find some handy advice about how to mark these practice papers. Make sure you've had a good read of it all before you get going.

Section A: Reading

1. 1 mark for ticking each of the following statements:
   - B Martin Bright was unhappy about the delay to his flight.
   - D Martin Bright began to think about how comfortable and relaxing travelling on the TGV would be.
   - E Martin Bright was told that some of the delay should be made up during the flight.
   - F Some of the passengers on the plane had problems with their seats.

2. When you're marking question 2, look at this table and work out which level description fits the answer best, then award the answer the mark you think it deserves from that level.

Number of marks	What's written	How it's written
7-8 marks Level 4	An in-depth understanding of the differences between the two methods of travelling.	Links the two texts in a perceptive way, including interpreting some implicit details. Chooses textual references that fully support points.
5-6 marks Level 3	A good understanding of the differences between the two methods of travelling.	Makes connections between the two texts and starts to analyse them. A range of relevant references to the texts are used to support points.
3-4 marks Level 2	Some differences between the two methods of travelling are pointed out.	Some attempts to make inferences and link the two texts together. Some points are supported by relevant references to the texts.
1-2 marks Level 1	Mentions simple differences between the two methods of travelling.	Paraphrases the texts and makes simple links between them. A few simple references to the texts are included.
0 marks	No differences given.	

Look for good points like these when you're marking:
- According to Text A, travelling by aeroplane is a stressful experience. Both writers describe how they cannot relax in an airport: Martin Bright complains that he cannot "genuinely relax" while waiting for his flight, and Vanessa Thorpe says that there is "no time to relax" in the airport. In contrast, Text B's writer finds travelling by stagecoach relaxing. His journey was filled with "repose and contentment", suggesting that it gave him a chance to unwind.
- Mark Twain's writing suggests that stagecoaches are a comfortable way to travel. He lies down "at full length" in the stagecoach, and can smoke the "pipe of peace" at leisure. Martin Bright's article gives the impression that aeroplane travel can be uncomfortable: he describes the "niggles" passengers have about "being too cold (or too hot)", and the "awkward" tables and arm rests. This view of plane travel is reinforced by Vanessa Thorpe's point that plane travel often leaves passengers with "aching ears and ballooned feet".
- For Twain, stagecoaching seems to be an exciting experience. He describes how he could feel his "sluggish pulses rousing" when at the top of the stagecoach, suggesting that his heart is beating faster in excitement. In contrast, Thorpe says that aeroplane travel has always "sapped" her "spirits". This suggests that it makes her feel lethargic and unhappy.
- Martin Bright says that "There is no way of making the journey part of the holiday" in reference to his flight to the south of France. This shows his purpose in flying: to get to the destination as quickly as possible, even if this means sacrificing some of his own comfort and enjoyment. Mark Twain however, talks of his journey as a "summer flight" and a "rare holiday frolic", showing how much he enjoyed it, and that the journey itself was part of the holiday rather than just the means of getting to his destination.

Set A — Paper 2

3   When you're marking question 3, look at this table and work out which level description fits the answer best, then award the answer the mark you think it deserves from that level.

Number of marks	What's written	How it's written
10-12 marks Level 4	In-depth and insightful analysis of the effects of a variety of language features.	Sophisticated technical terminology is used accurately. A perceptive selection of references to the text are used to support points throughout.
7-9 marks Level 3	The effects of a selection of relevant language features are all clearly explained.	Technical terminology is used accurately throughout the answer. A variety of suitable references to the text are used to support points throughout.
4-6 marks Level 2	Some language features are identified and their effects commented on.	Some technical terminology is used. Might not always be accurate. Some relevant references to the text are used to support some of the points.
1-3 marks Level 1	Limited understanding of language features, with occasional comment.	Simple or no use of subject terminology. May be inaccurate. Few points are supported by relevant references to the text.
0 marks	Nothing written about language.	

Look for good points like these when you're marking:

- Mark Twain uses onomatopoeia in the phrase "ceaseless rush and rattle and clatter" to evoke the sounds of the stagecoach journey to the reader. The repeated hard "t" sounds of "rattle" and "clatter" further emphasise the noise to the reader, which would help them to imagine how it sounded and felt to Mark Twain.
- Imagery is used to show the reader what the landscape looks like from the stagecoach. Twain uses the metaphor of a "grassy carpet" to describe the land, suggesting that it seems soft and luxurious like the carpet of a house. The imagery helps the reader to picture the scene, as well as share Twain's feelings of comfort and relaxation.
- Twain uses the senses to evoke the bodily experience of a person on the stagecoach: he describes his "sluggish pulses rousing" from the excitement caused by the stagecoach's speed. This helps the reader to feel as if they are on the stagecoach too, because they would understand that feeling from exciting experiences they've had themselves.

4   When you're marking question 4, look at this table and work out which level description fits the answer best, then award the answer the mark you think it deserves from that level.

Number of marks	What's written	How it's written
13-16 marks Level 4	A detailed, insightful comparison of the writers' attitudes, which demonstrates a perceptive understanding of the differences between the two viewpoints. In-depth analysis of the methods each writer uses to convey their point of view.	Points consistently supported by a good range of precise references to both texts.
9-12 marks Level 3	The writers' attitudes are clearly compared, showing a clear understanding of the differences between the two viewpoints. Answer includes relevant discussion of the methods used to convey both writers' ideas.	Appropriate references to both texts are used to support points.
5-8 marks Level 2	Some attempt to compare writers' attitudes, identifying some differences between their viewpoints and sometimes commenting on techniques used to convey them.	Includes references to the texts, but not always relevant.
1-4 marks Level 1	Basic identification of the two writers' attitudes and the differences between them, with only a limited awareness of the different ideas expressed in each text. Makes a few very simple references to methods used.	Some basic textual details or references, but many points are unsupported.
0 marks	Nothing written about the writers' attitudes.	

Look for good points like these when you're marking:

- Vanessa Thorpe's experience of train travel was almost entirely relaxing. Her use of the simile "as refreshed as if I had been lounging around on a sofa all day" compares her experience to that of an extremely relaxing day that most readers would be able to relate to. Mark Twain's experience however, seems to have been less relaxing overall. He acknowledges the "very comfortable" seats, but then goes on to use a very long, complex sentence (beginning "But then the conductor...") to list all the negative aspects of train travel. The length of the sentence makes the problems seem relentless to the reader, which reinforces Twain's frustration at the fact that he could not relax on the train.
- For his train journey, Mark Twain mentions that if you need to sleep, you can only do it "in naps". The adjectives he uses to describe his experience, "cramped" and "torturing", suggest extremes of pain and discomfort which help to convey the strength of Twain's feelings to the reader. Vanessa Thorpe doesn't write about her own attempts to sleep, but she uses a comparison — likening her journey to being on a "flying bed" — to convey the sense of comfort and the ease with which a passenger could fall asleep on the Eurostar train.

Set A — Paper 2

Section B: Writing

5
- Question 5 tests two things. There are 24 marks for having an interesting and well-organised answer ('Ideas and structure'), and 16 marks for good technical accuracy, including spelling, punctuation and grammar ('Quality of writing').
- Mark each of the criteria separately, then add up the two marks to get a total out of 40.
- The best answers also need to be really well-matched to the form, purpose and audience that are specified in the question.

	Ideas and structure		Quality of writing
19-24 marks Level 4	Imaginative use of structure and language techniques, thoroughly matched to form, purpose and audience. Engaging, well-developed, sophisticated ideas in well-controlled paragraphs.	13-16 marks Level 4	Ambitious use of vocabulary with highly accurate spelling; confidently uses a wide range of grammar and punctuation.
13-18 marks Level 3	Effective writing, using a clear structure and language techniques. Matched to form, purpose and audience. Interesting, clearly connected ideas in organised paragraphs.	9-12 marks Level 3	Largely suitable, varied vocabulary with accurate spelling; a range of mostly correct grammar and punctuation.
7-12 marks Level 2	Mostly matched to form, purpose and audience. Some language techniques and structural features. A range of ideas in logical paragraphs.	5-8 marks Level 2	Attempts a variety of vocabulary, punctuation and grammar, sometimes successfully. Some accurate spelling.
1-6 marks Level 1	Some sense of form, purpose and audience, with a mostly disorganised structure. A few relevant ideas in poorly controlled paragraphs.	1-4 marks Level 1	Simple vocabulary, grammar and punctuation are used with inaccuracies throughout. Basic spelling may be correct.
0 marks	Nothing meaningful written.	0 marks	Poor spelling, grammar and punctuation, which prevents understanding.

Look for good techniques like these when you're marking:
- Counter-argument: You could argue that plane travel is causing too much damage to the environment — but then you'd be ignoring all the advances in technology in recent years that have made planes much more fuel efficient.
- Satirical language: Of course, the most fantastic thing about aeroplanes is that they churn out pollutants that ruin the atmosphere and cause sea level to rise, threatening the livelihoods of people across the globe. So obviously it's great that we're using planes more and more.
- Statistics: Experts have proven that you are ten times safer in an aeroplane than on a train. The accident statistics for car travel are even more startling: you're nineteen times more likely to be killed when travelling by car than by plane.
- Rhetorical questions: Have you ever thought about how much more productive society is because we can move around so quickly? Do you think we'd ever get anything done if business leaders and world leaders all got the steamboat to their meetings on the other side of the planet?
- Repetition: If you think planes are dangerous, you are living in the past. If you think they are environmentally damaging then you are ill-informed. If you think that any other form of transport is more efficient, then you need to listen carefully to what I'm telling you in this article.
- Imagery: As trains plod through the landscape like tired old mules, planes canter through the sky like thoroughbred racehorses.

Set B — Paper 1

Before you start marking the Set B, Paper 1 practice exam, have a look at page 3 — you'll find some handy advice about how to mark these practice papers. Make sure you've had a good read of it all before you get going.

Section A: Reading

1 1 mark for ticking each of the following correct answers:
   1.1 Beneath the level of the forest floor
   1.2 Greenery
   1.3 Narrow
   1.4 A tree

2 When you're marking question 2, look at this table and work out which level description fits the answer best, then award the answer the mark you think it deserves from that level.

Number of marks	What's written	How it's written
7-8 marks Level 4	In-depth and insightful analysis of the effects of a variety of language features.	Sophisticated technical terminology is used accurately. A perceptive selection of references to the text are used to support points throughout.
5-6 marks Level 3	The effects of a selection of relevant language features are all clearly explained.	Technical terminology is used accurately throughout the answer. A variety of suitable references to the text are used to support points throughout.
3-4 marks Level 2	Some language features are identified and their effects commented on.	Some technical terminology is used. Might not always be accurate. Some relevant references to the text are used to support some of the points.
1-2 marks Level 1	Limited understanding of language features, with occasional comment.	Simple or no use of subject terminology. May be inaccurate. Few points are supported by relevant references to the text.
0 marks	Nothing written about language.	

Look for good points like these when you're marking:

- Descriptive verbs such as "leaned" and "peered" are used to show the old man's decrepit state. The adverb "heavily" used in conjunction with "leaned" betrays his reliance on his staff in order to move, whilst he peers at his feet, perhaps because he cannot see very far. These descriptions reinforce the idea of the old man's "extreme age".

- The adjectives "rude" and "mangy" used to describe the old man's skull-cap and garment show the rudimentary and poor state of his clothing. These words suggest that his clothes are simple, probably hand-made, and damaged, perhaps from being worn for many years, showing the reader how challenging his life has been.

- The long subordinate clause in the sentence beginning "His beard..." contrasts how the man's beard should have been ("snow-white") with how it really is (as stained as his "dirty-white" hair). This contrast emphasises to the reader how unkempt his appearance is, showing that he has probably lived outside for a long time, away from normal, civilised society.

- In the final sentence, the writer uses alliteration to highlight the man's age and experiences. The alliteration in "sunburn and scars and scratches" emphasises that he has many different marks on his body, caused by the many different dangers he has clearly encountered. This shows the reader that the man has had a hard life, but the fact that he has reached an "extreme age" shows that he must also be extremely hardy.

Set B — Paper 1

3   When you're marking question 3, look at this table and work out which level description fits the answer best, then award the answer the mark you think it deserves from that level.

Number of marks	What's written	How it's written
7-8 marks Level 4	Analyses the effects of a range of structural features confidently and in detail.	Sophisticated technical terminology is used accurately. Uses a perceptive range of examples from across the text.
5-6 marks Level 3	The effects of a variety of structural features are clearly explained.	Technical terminology is used accurately throughout. Suitable examples from the whole text are used and explained.
3-4 marks Level 2	The effects of some structural features are explained.	Some technical terminology is used. May not always be accurate. Some points are supported with relevant examples from the text.
1-2 marks Level 1	Basic attempts to comment on a few structural features in a simple manner.	Simple or no use of subject terminology. May be inaccurate. Few references are made to the text and are not always relevant.
0 marks	Nothing written about structure.	

Look for good points like these when you're marking:
- The text begins with a detailed description of the disused railroad. The richness of the description draws the reader into the world, but there is initially little sense of danger or threat. However, the final words of the first paragraph mention that the railroad is now a "wild-animal runway". This introduces an element of danger as it hints that there could be wild animals nearby.
- The writer then shifts the focus onto the characters in the story: an old man and a boy. The old man is described as "very old" and as needing a "staff" to walk — his frailty and the fact that he is on a "runway" used by wild animals increases the sense of danger and the reader fears for his safety. The young boy is clearly much fitter, but the text's description of him mentions both a "bow and an arrow" and a "hunting knife", which further heightens the sense of danger as it implies that the boy is expecting trouble.
- In the final paragraph, the pace quickens as the boy "Suddenly" becomes "alertly tense" and the reader immediately wonders what the danger is. The short sentences used in the first part of this paragraph contrast the long detailed descriptions of the previous paragraphs and mimic the quick decisions and actions of the characters. This builds tension for the reader and increases the sense of danger.

4   When you're marking question 4, look at this table and work out which level description fits the answer best, then award the answer the mark you think it deserves from that level.

Number of marks	What's written	How it's written
16-20 marks Level 4	In-depth, personal response to the statement, with critical, detailed analysis of the writer's choices.	Opinions are convincingly explained and fully supported with relevant, useful references to the text.
11-15 marks Level 3	Clearly explained response to the statement that discusses the effect of the writer's choices.	Opinions are clearly expressed and mostly supported with appropriate references to the text.
6-10 marks Level 2	An attempt at a personal response to the statement; some comments on the effect of the writer's methods.	Some opinions are explained and supported with references to the text.
1-5 marks Level 1	Limited response to the statement, with little mention of the effect of the writer's methods.	Only a few opinions are supported with relevant references to the text.
0 marks	Nothing written that responds to the statement.	

Look for good points like these when you're marking:
- I mostly agree that the writer creates a vivid portrayal of the boy. Imagery and detailed descriptions help the reader to visualise the boy, and give them clues about his life. For example, the simile "brown as a berry" might indicate that he has tanned skin, which would imply that he has spent a lot of time outside. His "catlike tread" suggests that he walks softly; by comparing the boy to an animal, the writer shows how attuned he is to life in the wild.
- The writer also focuses heavily on the boy's behaviour to build up the impression of what his life has been like. He studies his surroundings in a "habitual" way and his hearing has been trained to operate "automatically". The strong implication is that he is so used to having to be wary of his surroundings that he does it without thinking. This gives the reader a stark and interesting insight: he has clearly led a dangerous life.
- However, the writer does not give us the boy's name or any insights into his thoughts and feelings. The text focuses more on how the boy perceives the world — through his "acute" hearing, for example — rather than on who he is or what he's like. The reader is therefore unaware of the boy's personality, so the portrayal is not as vivid as it could be.

Set B — Paper 1

Section B: Writing

5
- Question 5 tests two things. There are 24 marks for having an interesting and well-organised answer ('Ideas and structure'), and 16 marks for good technical accuracy, including spelling, punctuation and grammar ('Quality of writing').
- Mark each of the criteria separately, then add up the two marks to get a total out of 40.
- The best answers also need to be really well-matched to the form, purpose and audience that are specified in the question.

	Ideas and structure		Quality of writing
19-24 marks Level 4	Imaginative use of structure and language techniques, thoroughly matched to form, purpose and audience. Engaging, well-developed, sophisticated ideas in well-controlled paragraphs.	13-16 marks Level 4	Ambitious use of vocabulary with highly accurate spelling; confidently uses a wide range of grammar and punctuation.
13-18 marks Level 3	Effective writing, using a clear structure and language techniques. Matched to form, purpose and audience. Interesting, clearly connected ideas in organised paragraphs.	9-12 marks Level 3	Largely suitable, varied vocabulary with accurate spelling; a range of mostly correct grammar and punctuation.
7-12 marks Level 2	Mostly matched to form, purpose and audience. Some language techniques and structural features. A range of ideas in logical paragraphs.	5-8 marks Level 2	Attempts a variety of vocabulary, punctuation and grammar, sometimes successfully. Some accurate spelling.
1-6 marks Level 1	Some sense of form, purpose and audience, with a mostly disorganised structure. A few relevant ideas in poorly controlled paragraphs.	1-4 marks Level 1	Simple vocabulary, grammar and punctuation are used with inaccuracies throughout. Basic spelling may be correct.
0 marks	Nothing meaningful written.	0 marks	Poor spelling, grammar and punctuation, which prevents understanding.

Look for good techniques like these when you're marking:

In a description:
- Metaphors: A waterfall of greenery cascaded down the towering cliff face.
- Similes: The tiger's face was framed by pure white tufts of fluffy hair; its eyes glowed like molten iron.
- Alliteration: Sharp, black slashes stretched across the tiger's russet coat.
- Language that appeals to the senses: There was a sweet, musky, almost soporific aroma in the warm air, its overpowering effect broken only by a low, guttural growl coming from the glaring tiger.

In the beginning of a story:
- An opening that directly addresses the reader: "Never smile at a crocodile", you might have heard people say. Well, I can tell you, I certainly wasn't smiling.
- Plenty of detail to bring the animal to life: The entire length of the crocodile's long snout was punctuated by a row of vicious, sharp teeth — sharp as switchblades. Glittering green scales covered the rest of its body, and sunlight danced off the droplets of water that rested upon them.
- Dramatic action to move the story on: I backed away hurriedly from the snapping jaws, pushing myself out of the water and up the sandy bank.
- A final sentence that makes the reader want to read on: As the crocodile glided away so innocently, I somehow knew that it would be back. Wounded as I was, all it had to do was wait for me to weaken further.

Set B — Paper 2

Before you start marking the Set B, Paper 2 practice exam, have a look at page 3 — you'll find some handy advice about how to mark these practice papers. Make sure you've had a good read of it all before you get going.

Section A: Reading

1   1 mark for ticking each of the following statements:
- A Miranda Sawyer thought that the butterfly bicycles were impressive.
- C The ceremony celebrated what people can achieve together.
- G Each petal that created the torch represented a different country.
- H Miranda Sawyer had a strong emotional reaction to the lighting of the torch.

2   When you're marking question 2, look at this table and work out which level description fits the answer best, then award the answer the mark you think it deserves from that level.

Number of marks	What's written	How it's written
7-8 marks Level 4	An in-depth understanding of the differences between the two opening ceremonies.	Links the two texts in a perceptive way, including interpreting some implicit details. Chooses textual references that fully support points.
5-6 marks Level 3	A good understanding of the differences between the two opening ceremonies.	Makes connections between the two texts and starts to analyse them. A range of relevant references to the texts are used to support points.
3-4 marks Level 2	Some differences between the two opening ceremonies are pointed out.	Some attempts to make inferences and link the two texts together. Some points are supported by relevant references to the texts.
1-2 marks Level 1	Mentions simple differences between the two opening ceremonies.	Paraphrases the texts and makes simple links between them. A few simple references to the texts are included.
0 marks	No differences given.	

Look for good points like these when you're marking:
- The performances in the 2012 ceremony aimed to celebrate the collective contribution of individuals to British society. In contrast, the 1851 exhibition opening primarily foregrounded the importance and superiority of the royal family. For example, in 2012 the spectacle consisted of different elements from multiple contributors, including a performance by NHS nurses, whereas the main performance spectacle of the 1851 exhibition was a royal procession.
- Music was a key feature of the two events, but the type of music played was very different. At the 2012 ceremony, modern pop music featured heavily. Emmy the Great "loved how much pop music featured" and Miranda Sawyer identifies pop stars who performed at the ceremony, such as Dizzee Rascal. At the 1851 exhibition opening, on the other hand, the music was only instrumental, provided by organs and a military band, as well as a "flourish of trumpets". It is implied that the music at the 1851 exhibition was used to create a grandiose atmosphere, whereas the 2012 opening ceremony was more focused on creating an upbeat and contemporary mood.
- The 2012 ceremony featured a variety of cultural icons, such as Tim Berners-Lee and Mr Bean. Although the Queen appeared, she was only one of the important figures featured. The main aspect of the 1851 exhibition opening was the appearance of Queen Victoria and Prince Albert at the "centre" of the Crystal Palace, suggesting that the ceremony was perhaps held to honour the royal family rather than celebrate a range of different public figures.
- The 2012 ceremony is made to sound informal and party-like, as Miranda Sawyer compares it to the "benevolent united madness" of Glastonbury. The noun "madness" especially makes it seem less ordered. The 1851 exhibition opening was more formal, including the "beautifully arranged" procession carried out to a "prescribed order" that was "exactly adhered to". This contrast between the two ceremonies may reflect the time periods in which they occurred, and the more formal way in which significant events were celebrated in the past.

Set B — Paper 2

3 When you're marking question 3, look at this table and work out which level description fits the answer best, then award the answer the mark you think it deserves from that level.

Number of marks	What's written	How it's written
10-12 marks Level 4	In-depth and insightful analysis of the effects of a variety of language features.	Sophisticated technical terminology is used accurately. A perceptive selection of references to the text are used to support points throughout.
7-9 marks Level 3	The effects of a selection of relevant language features are all clearly explained.	Technical terminology is used accurately throughout the answer. A variety of suitable references to the text are used to support points throughout.
4-6 marks Level 2	Some language features are identified and their effects commented on.	Some technical terminology is used. Might not always be accurate. Some relevant references to the text are used to support some of the points.
1-3 marks Level 1	Limited understanding of language features, with occasional comment.	Simple or no use of subject terminology. May be inaccurate. Few points are supported by relevant references to the text.
0 marks	Nothing written about language.	

Look for good points like these when you're marking:

- Queen Victoria uses imagery when she describes the crowd as "one mass of densely crowded human beings". The word "mass" accentuates the number of people there as it shows there were so many that Queen Victoria could not distinguish between them. This helps to convey to the reader some of the "bustle and excitement" of the event.
- Queen Victoria uses a list in the long, complex sentence beginning "The tremendous cheering..." to describe the event. Using a list in this way, Queen Victoria is able to convey the overwhelming nature of the event, as the quick succession of a long list of facts also leaves the reader feeling overwhelmed and breathless.
- Strong adjectives such as "magic" and "impressive" are used to show how amazing the scene was. The word "magic" especially suggests that it was so incredible it seemed unreal. Exaggerating the scene in this way sets the exhibition apart from other events, helping the reader to understand why it was "a day to live forever".

4 When you're marking question 4, look at this table and work out which level description fits the answer best, then award the answer the mark you think it deserves from that level.

Number of marks	What's written	How it's written
13-16 marks Level 4	A detailed, insightful comparison of the writers' attitudes, which demonstrates a perceptive understanding of the differences between the two viewpoints. In-depth analysis of the methods each writer uses to convey their point of view.	Points consistently supported by a good range of precise references to both texts.
9-12 marks Level 3	The writers' attitudes are clearly compared, showing a clear understanding of the differences between the two viewpoints. Answer includes relevant discussion of the methods used to convey both writers' ideas.	Appropriate references to both texts are used to support points.
5-8 marks Level 2	Some attempt to compare writers' attitudes, identifying some differences between their viewpoints and sometimes commenting on techniques used to convey them.	Includes references to the texts, but not always relevant.
1-4 marks Level 1	Basic identification of the two writers' attitudes and the differences between them, with only a limited awareness of the different ideas expressed in each text. Makes a few very simple references to methods used.	Some basic textual details or references, but many points are unsupported.
0 marks	Nothing written about the writers' attitudes.	

Look for good points like these when you're marking:

- Before the opening ceremony, Emmy the Great had a cynical attitude towards the Olympic Games. She uses short, angry exclamations such as "All the bloody adverts!" to show her complaints about the Games, and uses the metaphor "barriers of uninterest" to suggest unyielding walls and express to the reader how unlikely it was that the ceremony would excite her. Queen Victoria, on the other hand, has heard about people being cynical towards the exhibition, saying that there had been "so much opposition" to it, but she disagrees with these people, using strong adjectives such as "absurd" to describe their claims.
- Emmy the Great's attitude to the Olympics changes — ultimately, she feels much more positive about them. She describes the NHS scene as "brave", and she "loved" the pop music in the event. The ceremony helped her to "get excited" about the Olympics coming up, showing the strong impact it had on her. Queen Victoria expresses similar, positive sentiments about the 1851 exhibition opening. She describes the day as one of the "greatest and most glorious", using superlatives and alliteration to emphasise how happy and excited she is.

Set B — Paper 2

Section B: Writing

5
- Question 5 tests two things. There are 24 marks for having an interesting and well-organised answer ('Ideas and structure'), and 16 marks for good technical accuracy, including spelling, punctuation and grammar ('Quality of writing').
- Mark each of the criteria separately, then add up the two marks to get a total out of 40.
- The best answers also need to be really well-matched to the form, purpose and audience that are specified in the question.

	Ideas and structure		Quality of writing
19-24 marks Level 4	Imaginative use of structure and language techniques, thoroughly matched to form, purpose and audience. Engaging, well-developed, sophisticated ideas in well-controlled paragraphs.	13-16 marks Level 4	Ambitious use of vocabulary with highly accurate spelling; confidently uses a wide range of grammar and punctuation.
13-18 marks Level 3	Effective writing, using a clear structure and language techniques. Matched to form, purpose and audience. Interesting, clearly connected ideas in organised paragraphs.	9-12 marks Level 3	Largely suitable, varied vocabulary with accurate spelling; a range of mostly correct grammar and punctuation.
7-12 marks Level 2	Mostly matched to form, purpose and audience. Some language techniques and structural features. A range of ideas in logical paragraphs.	5-8 marks Level 2	Attempts a variety of vocabulary, punctuation and grammar, sometimes successfully. Some accurate spelling.
1-6 marks Level 1	Some sense of form, purpose and audience, with a mostly disorganised structure. A few relevant ideas in poorly controlled paragraphs.	1-4 marks Level 1	Simple vocabulary, grammar and punctuation are used with inaccuracies throughout. Basic spelling may be correct.
0 marks	Nothing meaningful written.	0 marks	Poor spelling, grammar and punctuation, which prevents understanding.

Look for good techniques like these when you're marking:
- Direct address: I'm sure everyone here today has seen the opening ceremony of an Olympic Games or another large event, and I imagine you'll agree that they're always very impressive. But isn't it all a bit of a waste of money?
- Emotive language: Organisers are throwing money away on pretty flashing lights while people are sweltering in broken-down train carriages in a desperate attempt just to get to the stadium.
- Rhetorical questions: Have you ever been stuck in a queue for several hours, only to find out all the tickets are gone?
- Varied sentence lengths: Opening ceremonies unite us all, reminding us of the things we have in common and what we might achieve. They inspire us.
- Repetition: Imagine the powerful, uplifting music. Imagine the excitement buzzing through the crowd. Imagine the fireworks lighting up the sky.
- Contrasts: Think about the trudge through the working week, and the crawl through 52 weeks of the working year. We all deserve to see something ridiculous and spectacular occasionally.